I READ! YOU READ!

Child's Turn to Read

Adult's Turn to Read

WE READ ABOUT
SEAHORSES

Amy Culliford and Madison Parker

TABLE OF CONTENTS

Words to Know 3
Sight Words 3
Index 16

SEAHORSE PUBLISHING

Parent and Caregiver Guide

Reading aloud with your child has many benefits. It expands vocabulary, sparks discussion, and promotes an emotional bond. Research shows that children who have books read aloud to them have improved language skills, leading to greater school success.

I Read! You Read! books offer a fun and easy way to read with your child. Follow these guidelines.

Before Reading

- Look at the front and back covers. Discuss personal experiences that relate to the topic.
- Read the *Words to Know* on page 3. Talk about what the words mean.
- If the book will be challenging or unfamiliar to your child, read it aloud by yourself the first time. Then, invite your child to participate in a second reading.

During Reading

 Have your child read the words beside this symbol. This text has been carefully matched to the reading and grade levels shown on the cover.

 You read the words beside this symbol.

- Stop often to discuss what you are reading and to make sure your child understands.
- If your child struggles with decoding a word, help them sound it out. If it is still a challenge, say the word for your child and have them repeat it after you.
- To find the meaning of a word, look for clues in the surrounding words and pictures.

After Reading

- Praise your child's efforts. Notice how they have grown as a reader.
- Ask and answer questions about the book.
- Discuss what your child learned and what they liked or didn't like about the book.

Most importantly, let your child know that reading is fun and worthwhile. Keep reading together as your child's skills and confidence grow.

WORDS TO KNOW

 color

 fins

 plankton

 seahorse

 tails

SIGHT WORDS

a	big	is	some
all	can	little	this
any	eat	long	
be	have	or	

This is a **seahorse**.

A **seahorse** is a type of fish that lives in the ocean.

A seahorse can be any **color**.

Seahorses can hide by changing their **color**. Special organs in their skin give them this ability.

Seahorses can be big or little.

The big-belly seahorse can be over one foot (30 centimeters) long.

All seahorses eat **plankton**.

Seahorses do not have teeth. They use their snouts to suck up **plankton**.

Some seahorses have long **tails**.

A seahorse can grip a plant or a rock with its **tail**. This keeps it from being swept away by the current.

All seahorses have **fins**.

A seahorse's **fins** help it move and swim in the water.

15

Index

big 8
color 6, 7
eat 10
little 8
long 8, 12
seahorse(s) 4, 5, 6, 8, 10, 12, 14

Written by: Amy Culliford and Madison Parker
Design by: Under the Oaks Media
Series Development: James Earley
Editor: Kim Thompson

Photos: Wildstrawberry: cover; Arunee Rodley: p. 5; Vojce: p. 7; Juliet Lisa Rose: p. 9; M-Production: p. 11; Andrea Izzotti: p. 13; Tim_Walters: p. 15

Library of Congress PCN Data
We Read About Seahorses / Amy Culliford and Madison Parker
I Read! You Read!
ISBN 979-8-8873-5185-8 (hard cover)
ISBN 979-8-8873-5205-3 (paperback)
ISBN 979-8-8873-5225-1 (EPUB)
ISBN 979-8-8873-5245-9 (eBook)
Library of Congress Control Number: 2022945540

Printed in the United States of America.

Seahorse Publishing Company
www.seahorsepub.com

Copyright © 2023 **SEAHORSE PUBLISHING COMPANY**

All rights reserved. No part of this publication may be reproduced, stored in a retrieval system or be transmitted in any form or by any means, electronic, mechanical, photocopying, recording, or otherwise, without the prior written permission of Seahorse Publishing Company.

Published in the United States
Seahorse Publishing
PO Box 771325
Coral Springs, FL 33077